Southern Sudan and Its Fight for Freedom

Santino Fardol

Bloomington, IN   authorHOUSE   Milton Keynes, UK

AuthorHouse™
1663 Liberty Drive, Suite 200
Bloomington, IN 47403
www.authorhouse.com
Phone: 1-800-839-8640

AuthorHouse™ UK Ltd.
500 Avebury Boulevard
Central Milton Keynes, MK9 2BE
www.authorhouse.co.uk
Phone: 08001974150

First published by AuthorHouse 6/8/2006

ISBN: 1-4259-3224-X (sc)

Printed in the United States of America
Bloomington, Indiana

This book is printed on acid-free paper.

Acknowledgements

First, I want to thank my wife for her support and my two wonderful sons for allowing me to use the computer while I was writing this book.

Many thanks and appreciation also go to my dear friends John and Mair Pugh, who are now living in Madagascar in Africa, for their great help and support and to my two friends Dr. Andrew Akon and Dr. Akec Khuc for their ideas.

Special thanks to my friend Philippe Geller, who helped me with useful references.

This book wouldn't have been in its present form if these people hadn't contributed to. Thank you, friends, for helping me make it what it is.

Preface

The war in Sudan has worsened and continues to do so at an alarming rate. As we watch the news on our TV screens or simply read the newspapers as we have done for the past 22 years in Darfur, Eastern Sudan, we are increasingly aware of the genocides of the people in Southern Sudan and other marginalised areas.

Slavery and holy war have been declared against the south. Millions have been killed or displaced to different parts of the world. Others have suffered humiliation, living in the worst human conditions in shantytowns around Khartoum and other northern major cities.

From day to day we fear that many more are going to become victims in the air raids carried out by government warplanes or militants loyal to the government. Indeed, our country is being destroyed and torn apart by those in the north claiming to be Arabs, and their successive governments.

As mistreated and humiliated citizens, we have responded for many years with political dialogue in order to settle our differences. We have tried peaceful means but failed to attain our goals (self-determination). We have also acted militarily (wars) and paid a heavy price. It is now time to put an end to the suffering of our people once and for all, and this is what this book is about.

The aim of this book is to explain to the loyal citizens of Southern Sudan the importance of voting "yes" to the separation of the south in the referendum, and saying no to a unified Sudan an old objective that has been the desire of our people for centuries.

It also endeavours to dispel any misunderstandings about the unity of the south, which certain politicians and ordinary people in south have somewhat miscalculated.

Southerners, and the whole world, need to know and understand why voting in the referendum for the separation of Southern Sudan is so crucial.

To give an accurate answer to this question, one would need to review some historical events that have played a significant role in Sudanese problems today.

As some writers have already put it, many agreements and promises have been broken or dishonoured by successive governments in Khartoum. Millions of southerners have been killed and buried in mass graves, displaced or taken captive as slaves, not to mention endured many other kinds of human sufferings such as the elimination or assassination of southern leaders (politicians who did not agree with these regimes).

This book also aims to explain to our people how well off we will be without the north if we all choose separation.

Study carefully the six reasons why we must obtain an independent Southern Sudan.

By Santino F. Watod

Introduction

In order to better understand the roots of our problems, one must first review some of the country's past events.

The civil war in Sudan began in 1983, when southern Sudanese rebels launched what was known as a national revolution against the dominant north, demanding their own government. Since then, three million have died, with nearly five million people internally displaced and living under the worst human conditions in Khartoum suburbs (shanty towns) and in some major northern cities. Nearly a million are refugees in neighbouring countries and around the world[1].

An unknown number of our people are still held in slavery or in captivity in the north, yet no one seems to care about them.

Many innocent people have died as a result of direct killing by the Sudanese Army and its militia or as a result of indirect killing through a

[1] For the figures see Bona Malwal's latest book, Sudan's Latest Peace Agreement, page 11

policy of famine, drawn up by the government, to deny access to food for the southern Sudanese population.

This policy was a means of fighting the Sudanese People's Liberation Army/Movement (SPAL/M) and extending, by force, the northern agenda of Islamization and Arabization.

Since Sudan gained its independence from the British on the 1st of January 1956, the northerners have dominated the political arena of the country and made Islam the only legal religion (law), ignoring all other religions, including Christianity and other local beliefs.

Orders, changes in government, education policies, and money all come from Khartoum.

For centuries, the north has denied the southern Sudanese any means of livelihood. Little or no access has been granted to health care, media, or higher education such as university. In fact, only a small number of southern students have managed to work their way into the University of Khartoum, some were later expelled for political reasons.

Since independence, no new roads have been built or even planned in the south. All the southern roads and institutions in the south date back to the colonial era.

In February 1983, Joseph James Tumbura wrote a secret petition to President Nimeiri demanding the immediate division of South Sudan[2] On the 5th of June 1983, Nimeiri went beyond all limits to violate the Addis Ababa Agreement by dividing the Southern Region into the three regions of Bahr el Ghazal, Equatoria and Upper Nile, thus weakening us even further.

This action was in gross violation of Article 8 of the Constitution of 1973 and Article 2 of the Addis Ababa Agreement[3].

Being supported by some southern politicians, Nimeiri went on implementing the Sharia laws in October 1983.

As all the country's economic and natural resources—oil, gold, and fertile lands for farming are located in the south, the northerners have demarcated the country, annexing the wealthy areas of Southern Sudan to the north.

The northern attitudes against the south continued and led the people of the south to finally realise that the only way to deal with these policies was to take up arms and conduct a war that would give them the right to break away from the north. A decision that is still in question.

---

[2] Dr. Lam Akol, SPLM/SPLA, Inside an African Revolution, page 11.
[3] Dr Lam Akol, SPLM/SPLA, Inside an Africa Revolution, page 7.

I and those who joined me in the bush and fought for more than twenty years, have brought to you CPA (Comprehensive Peace Agreement) in a golden plate. Our mission is accomplished. It is now your turn, especially those who did not have a chance to experience bush life. When time comes to vote at referendum, it is your golden choice to determine your fate. Would you like to vote to be second-class citizens in your own country? It is absolutely your choice.

Dr John Garang de Mabior

Rumbek, Southern Sudan.

May 15, 2005

As I write, the war is not yet over. Our country continues to suffer from the killing of intellectuals and the racism and domination of the north.

When the referendum comes, make no mistake about your/our future.

The secession of Southern Sudan is the only option that the SPLA/M leaders must opt for; otherwise, the civil war is likely to continue, particularly if they and their northern partners try to renege on their commitments.

We must demand that our leaders jump through a new set of hoops. The idea of unity must be written off.

Contents

1.
A brief history of the Sudan

Sudan is one of the largest African countries, neighbouring nine other countries: Egypt, Libya, Chad, Central African Republic, Uganda, Democratic Republic of Congo (formerly Zaire), Kenya, Ethiopia, and Eritrea.

Sudan encompasses 2,505,813 square kilometres, with a land area of 2,376,000 square kilometres and a coastline of 716 kilometres. Its internal problems are bigger than its size. The country achieved its independence from the Anglo-Egyptians on the 1st of January 1956.

By July 1990, the population was estimated to be approximately 25 million.

Sudan has waged many painful internal wars since its independence. For this reason, its citizens, as well as the international community, tend to question what exactly went wrong with this huge country. Many have already explained why Sudan has experienced so many internal problems. I am merely explaining them again, as a witness to what has already been said.

Of course, those who dare to seek out the truth behind the conflicts and wars are absolutely right to ask such questions. Many things have gone wrong in this vast country. So let's take a few steps to explain what indeed went wrong.

The country underwent foreign occupation for three devastating periods: the entrance of Islam, the invasion of the Turco-Egyptians, and the Anglo-Egyptian invasion

Islam entered Sudan in about 700 AD, brought by the invading Christian kingdoms of Nubian, Merwe, Mekuria, Soba, and Alwa, which were prospering at that time. This period lasted over a thousand years. Following the Islamic period came the invasion of the Turco-Egyptians, whose rule lasted from 1820 to 1885.

The Turco-Egyptian has been described as cruel and inhumane. The aim of this second invasion was to collect slaves (blacks) and gold.

The Turco-Egyptians, together with some northern Sudanese Arab traders such as Zubier Rahama, conducted raids into the southern territories looking for both slaves (abids/abeeds) and gold. The slave trade continued and became worse during the Mahdist state from 1885 to 1898.

The third wave of foreign invasion was led by the Anglo-Egyptians in 1898 under Lord Kitchner, ending the Mahdist state. During the Anglo-Egyptian period, from 1898 to 1956, the country was divided into two separate administrations both under the Governor General. The British administration realised that an inequality existed between the north and south as well as other parts of the country. To protect the indigenous African populations, the British introduced a new concept known as closed districts for three areas: Southern Sudan, the Nubian Mountains, and the Southern Blue Nile. The act of closing up these areas was a clear indication by the British administration that there was a need to protect these people from wrong practices such as slavery, Islamisation and Arabisation.

In 1947, some years before independence, the British conspired with several Arabian countries, especially Egypt, as well as Arabs in northern Sudan to reverse the policy of protection offered by the closed districts. They decided to unify the south and the north instead of allowing the people of these closed districts the right to self-determination.

I believe that the British policy of the closed districts was upheld and endorsed by these indigenous populations; unfortunately, the administration did not keep its word.

The result of this history essentially divided the country into two: the northern part, dominated by Arabs and Muslims, and the Southern part, all of whom are indigenous African tribes and the majority of whom are Christian.

The division is distinct in linguistic, religious, racial, and even economic fields.

The long slave trade practiced by the north against the south and others factors created during the colonial period, such as the failure to let the people of the closed districts determine their own future, generated two painful civil wars.

The first started with Anyana I on the 18th of August 1955 and ended with the Addis Ababa's Agreement in 1972. The second war with the Sudan Peoples' Liberation Army/Movement (PSLA/M) started in 1983 and ended on the 9th of January 2005 with the signing of the Peace Accord in Nairobi, Kenya.

These factors, as well as many others, have affected and continue to affect the lives of citizens both politically and economically.

2.

What really provoked the first civil war?

As I have already mentioned, the south despises the north because of the long history of the slave trade and the failure of the northern elite and their governments to address and solve national issues in a peaceful way. On the contrary, the northern leaders continue to lead the country into mass suffering even today.

In 1947, at the Juba Conference, the call for the right to self-determination by the people of the south was denied. Elders such as Chief Lolik led the southern delegation and demanded the following from the Anglo-Egyptians:

1. The south should be granted a period of ten years during which it can develop in all fields, including civil services and education, in order to catch up with the development in the north; and

2. After reaching the same level of

devolvement as the north, the south should be able to decide its own fate, whether to remain a part of Sudan or to join East Africa or become an independent state.

These demands were rejected by the northern elite simply because they did not serve their interests of continuing to exploit southerners and their resources. Moreover, it prevented them from attaining their goal of Islamising the south and making us Arabs. Clear evidence of the north's interest in the south is the deal of the Arabs in then north along with the Anglo-Egyptians in 1953 that gave the country its independence without consulting the people of Southern Sudan. Southern Sudanese people have never believed that they obtained their independence. They believe that white colonials were simply replaced by black colonials (Arabs).

The reason behind this conspiracy between Egyptians and the northern Sudanese was rights to the Nile's water. Egypt continues to manipulate the north for the same interest, calling the Sudanese "habna al nil" (the sons of the Nile). Being both Arabs and Muslims, they were able to make their own pacts with each other, even though the sharing of the water of the Nile remains overwhelmingly in favour of Egypt[4].

---

[4] Bona Malwal, Sudan's Latest Peace Agreement page 21

After the British decided to re-annex the south to the north, southerners were extremely angry. They knew that replacing the British colonials with northern Arabs was disastrous. Being side by side with the north was not going to bring anything but hardship, slavery, and discrimination.

Furthermore, the northerners were only interested in taking southern land and turning it into a source of food for the Arab states.

From 1954 to 1955, in accordance with the agreements made in Cairo between the northerners and the Anglo-Egyptians the year before, the Arabs in the north took over both the civil administration and the power from the colonials. This led to doubts amongst the southerners, which led them to start asking themselves questions such as whether one day the south would really become free. These doubts were rooted in the belief that southerners are slaves (abids/abeeds) and infidels who need to be converted to Islam by whatever means possible —by force, by buying them with money, or by giving them positions.

There was no doubt that the south had to resist these long-term goals of the north. As a result, protests broke out all over the southern regions against the new colonial Arabs of northern Sudan. Those protesters were absolutely right; the north would deny our right to freedom, which history has witnessed.

These feelings resulted in the Torit mutinies on the 18th of August 1955 and again on the 16th of May 1983 in Bor.

Our elders' predictions came true; their fears were based on the fact that northern politicians were only concerned with fulfilling their own interests. We have lived in such a state since 1955.

The northerners bought some of our politicians during the Juba Conference on the 12th of July 1947.

They cheated or were bribed to hold high positions in the local or national government; some of them received gifts of money, promotions, or luxury items in order to support and accept the unity of Sudan. Some were decorated with false decorations, such as "awlad el balad or Watunyi" (watunyyi is Arabic for patriotic). This was great mistake for which the south paid eight years later in Anyanya I on the 18th of August 1955 and again in 1983 at the SPLA/M.

Those politicians who were wise and knew the game understood the real situation. They were opposed the idea of a marriage between the south and the north, aware of what the north was really after. These politicians were later assassinated by the government or served long sentences in prison, including the recent assassinations of Dr. John Garang de Mabior on the 30th of July 2005 (see chapter 7) as well as that of William Deng Nahil.

Nahil, secretary general of the Sudan African National Union (SANU), was assassinated near Rumbek by the very Umma party leaders who wanted him to work for them in 1965.The truth about his assassination remains hidden beneath a shroud of secrecy.

In order to maintain their rule in Sudan, northerners adapted a policy drawn up by the Anglo-Egyptians called "divide and rule." This policy has been very efficient and productive for the northern elite politicians, dividing the country so that they can rule it without difficulty. Taking advantage of the diversity of the south, which is composed of hundreds of different local tribes, they turned the minorities against the majority tribes and vice versa. They offered higher positions to tribes spoke out against Dinka domination or Nuer against Shiluk or Dinka Bor —in short to serve their interest of Arabization and Islamization of the country.

The clearest example of such instigated rivalry was the differences between Joseph Lagu[5] from the Madi tribe in the Equatoria region and

---

[5] Lagu was a leader of Anyana I who led the army struggle against the government in Khartoum for 17 years. After the Addis Ababa Peace Accord, he became a major general in the Sudanese Army.

Abel Alier[6], a Dinka from Bor in the Upper Nile region. The contradiction between these two dominating leaders related to and reflected the differences and conflicts within the Southern society[7].

The objection of the south to these sabotages led southerners to stage the Torit uprising of the 18th of August 1955. This uprising was viewed in the north as a further attempt by southerners to break away from the north. The prime minister at that time, Ishmael El Azhari, was one of the worst prime ministers in Sudan's history.

He thought the only way to deal with this uprising and bring the south under control was by suppressing the south.

Numerous massacres were approved and conducted against people in the South simply because they were demanding nothing more than their own legitimate rights. In 1955 in Torit alone (Torit is a town in southern Sudan in Equatoria), northern supporters killed more them 1,000 men and women.

On the 9th of July 1965 in Juba, thousands of southerners were massacred by the government's army. Just two days later, on the 11th of July in

[6] Alier is a trained lawyer who served as the president of the High Executive of Southern Sudan from April 1972 to the 1st of July 1978.
[7] Sharif Harir and Terje Tvedt, Short-cut to Decay: The case of the Sudan page 72.

Wau,[8] many wedding party guests were massacred by the government army. The July 1965 massacres of the educated southern elite in both Wau and Juba bore testimony to the changed attitude and policy of the central government towards the South[9]. For the names of those killed in Wau, see the list at the back of this book (list N°1).

In modern society, an army is charged with protecting the nation and its citizens from outside aggression; in Sudan, however, citizens from marginalised areas are the prime targets for the army and national police.

The killing of 24 Dinka chiefs held in detention in Bor was another cleaning up operation by the Arabs. The chiefs had been arrested following the death of a single Northern Sudanese army officer, Lieutenant Bayoumi, who was killed by Anyanya forces on the battlefield. The government believed that the Anyanya forces lived within the community and that the chiefs must have been aware of the fact. When the chiefs refused to divulge their alleged knowledge, the detainees included the paramount chief of the Bor district, Ajang Duot[10].

---

[8] Wau is the capital Province of Bhar el Ghazal

[9] Sharif Harir & Terje Tvedt, Short-cut to Decay/the case of the Sudan page 105.

[10] See Dr. Mansour Khalid (1990: 218) for the details of the incident and "Sudan Democratic Gazette," April 2001, page 4.

The assassination of Father Saturnio[11] in 1966 occurred when Iberahim Abdoud was in power. Father Saturino was arrested in Uganda by authorities and taken across the border into Southern Sudan, where he was handed over to the Sudanese army. He was then tortured to death and his body was riddled with bullets in preparation for the cover-up story put out by the government in Khartoum.

In May 1969, General Jaafar Mohammed Nimeiri seized power in a military coup d'état. As a northerner, his desire was to crack down on the National Liberation Movement in the south by military means. Despite his efforts using all possible logical means and military support from abroad, mainly from Arab countries, he gave up his military fight, realising that the only solution to the north-south conflict was through political channels.

Indeed, the reward for his efforts was the Addis Ababa Peace Accord of February 1972 with the Anyanya military wing of the movement led by Colonel Joseph Lagu.

This peace agreement was widely rejected and denounced by certain politicians and military of-

[11] According to investigation carried out by some southern politicians, it was revealed that Father Saturnio died as a result of a secret agreement between Prime Minister Milton Obote of Uganda and Khartoum to round up the leaders of the southern rebellion. "Sudan Democratic Gazette," April 2001, page 3.

ficers as a fraud and sell out, which did not serve the cause. One of these outspoken leaders was the late hero Garang de Mabior, then the leader of the SPLA/M and former first vice-president.

Some regarded it as another attempt by the north to disarm the Anyanya, who were making significant gains on the ground. Under the agreement, the south was granted regional autonomy with some limited power and the absorption of approximately 6,000 Anyanya I guerrillas into the national army and the police and prison services (the exact number is not known). In fact, there was no single word that guaranteed the agreement against further fraud, such as abrogation by the government, which was one of the mistakes made by those who signed the agreement.

The Addis Ababa Agreement neither met our dream and satisfaction of self- determination nor gave us equal rights in sharing the power with the north.

When the northerners were sure that they had deprived the south of everything, Nimeiri accelerated the programme of Islamisation and Arabisation of the country. Much land was seized in the south and many more mosques were built with the help of Islamic organisations such as the International Dawa Islamia Organisation.

Nimeiri did away with every single right that was given to the southerners in the Addis Ababa Agreement, finally abrogating the entire agreement in June 1983 when he divided the south into three states (Bhar el Ghazal, Equatoria and Upper Nile). He continued to poison the attitudes of northerners toward the south by annexing southern oil fields to the north.

When Nimeiri was sure he had made progress in installing the north's agenda into practice and was decorated by the north and the Arab countries for his achievements, he made himself an Imam. In September 1983 he implemented the Islamic Sharia as the (heavenly) law for the country, ignoring other religions and cultures.

The abrogation of the accord, division of the south into three regions, annex of the southern lands to the north, acceleration of Islamisation and Arabisation, and Sharia frustrated our people and led to the outbreak of hostilities in major cities.

On the 16th of May 1983, Nimeiri's forces attacked one of its own units.

Nimeiri introduced the kasha (Arabic word meaning rounding up through the use of police force) in September 1981.

During Nimeiri's rule and the coalition government of Ashdiq from 1986 to 1989, southerners and other people (blacks) from marginalised areas were still being arrested and deported in what was known to all Sudanese as kasha. I share my own experiences as I am one of those victims.

In Matha al usta (the central station) in Khartoum several southern students (myself included) from Maridi higher Secondary School were apprehended by the special police force, known as Difah madeny, and taken to the Khartoum police general headquarters. It was a bad day for me as well as for my colleagues, for I personally had not been arrested before. I was not surprised for I had expected at some point to be arrested like innocent southerners, Nubians, or Darfurians, because that was the reality facing us. Whenever a black man or woman wore civilian clothes, he or she was the prime target for kasha, even those who worked in the government, who were also targeted when wearing civilian clothes.

Arriving at the police headquarters, the lone southern officer on duty managed to secure my release.

The rest of my colleagues remained in jail till the next day and were only released when the headmaster of the school intervened. What contributed to my release was that I was very sick; I had the chickenpox and a fever. Maybe the Arab officers feared my health would deteriorate, causing them a lot of trouble.

Whatever the reason, I thank my brother from the south because he sacrificed himself in order to have his brother released. I am sure I was not the only one. He might have done that several times and on different occasions.

The policy of "divide and rule" divided our people for very long time. I personally do not blame the illiterate who accepted and collaborated with the Arabs; but I do blame those politicians who knew the truth about the northerners' interests and yet were happy to work with the Arabs. (Some continue to collaborate with the Arabs.) —Shame on our politicians who served the Arab's agenda and those tribes that accepted misleading actions from people who only seek to achieve their own objectives without looking deeply into the roots of the differences between the people of the south and the north.

Let me cite some of those differences now, both naturally and geographically. The north is a desert while the south is a forest. In the north, despite the rejection by other Arab countries that the Sudanese are not Arabs, the majority in the North claim to be Arabs and Muslims, while we in the south are pure African and Christian.

At the point, I would like to acknowledge that in the south a small number still believe in local religions, and we do have a small number of Muslim brothers and sisters. If I happened to be one of those politicians, I would look deeply into those roots and would accept my brother from the Latuka tribe who both is an African and Christian/Muslim, rather than accepting someone who considers himself to be my master and who imposes a single identity on the entire country without taking into consideration the internal cultural composition of the Sudanese population. I would choose to live poor and clean rather than sell out my dignity, my people, and my country. I would also choose to establish a dialogue with my brother from Equatoria, the Upper Nile, or from Bhar El Ghazal to settle our differences peaceably.

This policy of division and disunity has had a significant impact on Sudanese politics and has generated great harm for its citizens as well as the country's economy.

3.

Southern resistance to the occupation

In 1820, Mohammed Ali Pasha conquered Sudan and annexed it to the Turco-Egyptian Ottoman Empire. The empire was facing many challenges, from war to economic issues; fearing the collapse of their empire, they sought to maintain its expansion.

To deal with these matters, they had to find the ways and means they needed to remain powerful both militarily and economically in order to challenge the European powers of the time, such as Great Britain. Of course, Pasha thought of Sudan because the country had what he needed: economic and human resources (gold and men). Soon after invading and defeating the Sudanese, Pasha sent his son to the south to look after the gold and slaves.

When the Turco- Egyptians came to Sudan, the slave- trade was only practiced in the south of the country by the northerners (the first bar-

barian act by the north against the south) and some Europeans. The victims, of course, were southerners, Nubians, and all blacks in general.

Despite the Anglo-Egyptian effort to abrogate this trade, it continued throughout the period of the Turco-Egyptian rule (from 1820 to 1884), through the period of the Anglo-Egyptian rule (from 1885 to 1898), and on into the present time. Although the Anglo-Egyptians may argue this assertion, even during the Anglo-Egyptian rule, southerners were slaves in the form of domestic and agricultural labour.

During these two periods of colonial occupation, southerners fought in the thousands along side the northerners to defeat the occupation. Yet their names and brave acts were not even written down or mentioned in the fabricated history of Sudan! One name alone —Chol, a Dinka from Ahlib known in the history books as Ali Abda al tif (some said his father was a Nubian and his mother a Dinka woman) —was included.

I use his real name because I do not believe that he had accepted Islam as his religion of choice. He was given the name of Ali after his death in order to proclaim the superiority of Muslims in the liberation of Sudan, who alone liberated Sudan (with some help from the northerners). Similarly, Arok Thun Arok was decorated and given a Muslim name after he was killed in Bentiew by the Sudanese government, which claimed that his plane had crashed in Bentiew (an unconfirmed claim said he was killed by Zuiber's bodyguards), killing Arok and 24 others on the 12th of February 1998. The current Sudanese Foreign Minister, Dr Lam Akol, and 14 others survived.

Chol was a former army officer and founder of the first nationalist movement in 1921. He united the country, calling for an independent Sudan in which power was shared.

His ideas were copied by the northern elites, who betrayed him to the British saying, "British, look, these people (the southerners) are bad, can't you see it by yourselves?

What ideas they have against you! When you leave, please give us the power so that we can protect your interests and ourselves." Chol was arrested and exiled to Egypt. The same people who discredited him later used his brilliant ideas.

4.

Why do we need to be independent?

In my opinion, six facts oblige us to break away from the north:

1. Northern Sudanese have exploited our ancestors, continue to exploit us today, and consider us as slaves (abeed) or second-class citizens. As long as we live together, their mentality will never change.

2. They are only interested in taking our land and exploiting our resources for their benefits.

3. They do not like when we assert ourselves as Africans and Christians, not Arabs. They want to change our identity, turning us into Arabs and Muslims by any means.

4. We have nothing in common with the cultures or religion of the north.

5. We should never allow them again to kill (Jihad), divide, or exploit us.

6. They have been betraying or violating every single agreement signed in the past; we should not trust them any more.

Looking to these facts and what I have already mentioned, we do not have anything in common with the north that would bind us together. Moreover, we are fed up with the false promises made by their elders and their elites.

Why should we continue to suffer? After all, ten years from now we are likely to pay another high price. Why must good gestures always come from the south and not from the north? Why can we not become our own masters and lead ourselves in a united south, where we will no longer hear someone calling "yah abeed" (you slave) or "janubiy" (Arabic word for southerner).

We will be better off without the north. The propaganda that the northern elite has always applied to divide us is already well known and will no longer brain wash southerners about choosing unity.

We must reject by an overwhelming majority their old fashion Wihda el Sudan (Sudan's unity). Are you ready to take part in this historical change in the favour of Southern Sudan's future, where our coming generation will live in a country of their own and have full freedom?

Let me take you through this little journey. I am going to give you some evidence of what serious damage and crimes have been committed against Southern Sudan and the southerners (I said some because no one knows full record of the crimes committed by the north against the southerners) and then leave it to you to judge and understand why we need to have our own state.

From the Turco-Egyptian colonial times up to the present day, we have suffered from the slave-trade. Your brothers and sisters from various regions of the south (mostly from Bhar Al Ghazal) were taken as slaves by force; some are still being taken as slaves and continue to be captives in the north. Some were sold to European and Arabian countries where they served both as slaves and soldiers and never came back.

A great number of our fellow countrymen ended up fighting along side the French Empire in Mexico in 1862 during the time of Emperor Napoleon the III[12].

- Although slavery was abolished a long time ago, it is still in the minds of many northerners, who still use it today to degrade us. Those who have studied the Arabic language or the fabricated history of the Sudan read about Zubeir Wad

[12] A Black Corps d'Elite, by Richard Hill and Peter Hogg, page, 17.

Ramah[13], who was in charge of the slave-trade mainly around Bhar Al Ghazal in Raga, Dimzuber. Do you know how many innocent citizens of the south he personally killed? Read "Black Ivory" by Jackson and you will find out where he testified.

- The killing of more than 1,000 people in Torit in 1955.

- On the 9th of July 1965 in Juba, they killed thousands of our men, women, and children (some estimates put it over 6,000 people).

- On the 11th of July in the same year in Wau they massacred an entire wedding party, including the bride and groom, see the list of names at the back of this book (list N° 1).

- The murdering of 24 Dinka chiefs in detention in Bor.

- The assassination of William Deng Nihal in 1965[14] and Father Saturino in 1966.

- The slaughter of more than 100 Dinka men and women on the 18 of July 1987

[13] Zubeir is from the north Khartoum Jilly. He was a master trader of slaves in Bhar El Ghazal. Dimzuber town was named after him. In Khartoum, capital of Sudan, the government of the north decided to name a street after him.

[14] For more details about the killing of Mr. Deng see Alier, Southern Sudan Too Many Agreements Dishonoured, page 107.

in Zagalona, north of the Wau military base, by the Sudanese Army (the 311th Field Artillery Battalion)[15].

- In 1989, the slaughter of more than 1,000 Shilluks men and women by the Sabaha Ta' aisha Baqqara in Jebelein. The Jebelein incident was initiated by an Arab landowner who demanded that his Shilluk field hands return to work on the last day of their Christmas celebration. In the ensuing altercation the Omda was killed, the slaughter proceeded immediately[16].

- On the 3rd of August 1987, Major General Abu Gurun supervised a search of Dinka quarters that resulted in the death of more than 100 Dinka in Wau. In addition, hundreds were taken to the Jur River (also called Nar al Jur), where they were shot and thrown to the crocodiles[17].

- On the 6th of September 1987, the killing of 25 of our police in Wau and the death of more than 300 civilians at the hands of the Sudanese Army[18].

[15] Source Requiem for the Sudan War, Drought, Disaster Relief on the Nile, J. Millard Burr and Robert O. Collins page, 223.
[16] For more details see Requiem for the Sudan War, Drought, Disaster Relief on the Nile/J. Millard Burr and Robert O. Collins page 264.
[17] Source Requiem for the Sudan War, Drought, Disaster Relief on the Nile, J. Millard Burr and Robert O. Collins page, 91.
[18] Source Requiem for the Sudan War, Drought, Disaster Relief on the Nile, J. Millard Burr and Robert O. Collins page, 91.

- On the 11th of September 1991, they poisoned Brigadier Pio Yukwan Deng. (Although not officially declared, I believe he was a victim of northern politicians. He was killed because he said in the days of their dirty revolution that, if the revolutionaries proved to have a link with the Islamic Front, he would resign from the Revolution Council.)

- El Dien's massacre on the 27th of March 1987. More than 1,000 of our brothers and sisters from Dinka (all from Aweil county, where I come from) were gathered in a freight train and told by the police that they were going to be protected from the Arab Baggara[19]. The police made sure that there was no one left outside before allowing the Baggara and Raziyqat Arabs to come in and set fire to the train, killing all the refugees, while the police looked on[20]. It is believed that the police even participated in the massacre with logistical equipment such as petrol.

- The execution of our men after attempt to capture Juba by SPLA forces in 1992 (see the names at the back of this book,

[19] The Baggara and Rizayqat are one of the Arabs group that support the Umma party
[20] For more details, you can read Requiem for the Sudan War, Drought, and Disaster Relief on the Nile, J. Millard Burr and Robert O. Collins page, 81

list N° 2)

- The killing of retired army brigadier and former governor of Eastern Equatoria, Camillo Odongi Loyuk, who was tortured to death by the regime's secret agents.

- The recent killing of our legend and the late hero Garang de Mabior on the 30th of July 2005 and mowing down of many innocent civilians in various cities after his death.

- Massacres of our innocent children, mother, and men in Cairo, Egypt, at one of the public parks in the Al-Muahandiseen quarter on New Year's Eve 2005. Many analysts believe that the Sudanese government was behind the massacres.

Ashdiq El Madi prime minister of the third democratic government, denied all the implications in the El Dien's massacre.

During Ashadiq's debate in Paris on the 7th of April 2005, he explained his party's position regarding the UN Council Resolutions 1551 and 1593, stating that his Umma party supported these two resolutions.

When he gave the chance to those attending to ask questions (only for two minutes), I asked him "Mr. Ashadiq, as I understood you and your Umma party support the setting up of the International Criminal Court and agreed with the UN resolution that calls for the criminals of war in Darfur to be brought before this court for justice. Are you and your party not aware that your decision would betray you personally because you are a criminal of war yourself? Don't you remember that you killed many people in Sudan, especially southerners?

I started recounting all crimes in which he had been personally involved, starting with the killing of Deng Nihal in 1965 and ending with the El Dien's massacre 1987, when he was Prime Minister. Ashadiq admitted his party involvement in the killing of Nihal, saying that he personally regretted the killing. He also added that, when the incident occurred and he asked then-Prime Minister Mohammed Ahmed Magub why the decision was taken without consulting him as the party leader, his asking was considered to be an offence that started a conflict between himself and Magub

He went on to deny his party's implications in the El Dien's massacre. I believe Ashadiq was lying. He and his northern politicians intended to kill eminent leaders and southern intellectuals who were opposed to the collaboration.

The numbers of southerners killed by northerners during the two conflicts as well as since the conflicts are staggering, and no one knows exactly how many millions have been killed or when exactly these genocides happened.

From 1985 to 1986, I was still in Wau and what I witnessed (as I do believe many of you witnessed in some areas across the south) is that southerners, mainly from Dinka and Jur, were the main targets for the Sudanese Army. They were shot down by soldiers who claimed that these civilians were from the SPLA or their families served in the movement. Young girls and women were raped; houses, hospitals, and public places were raided by soldiers. Such crimes against our people happened throughout the south clearly a genocide carried out by Arabs to frighten us so that we would surrender and kneel before them.

Their calculation was wrong. We, the people of Southern Sudan, will never bow before them and surrender like chickens being chased! We will always demand our rights in peaceful ways; if these demands are not met, we will use necessary force and make many sacrifices. The language of war is the only language that they understand, so war must continue, in its form, until we are totally free.

We are not afraid to die either. Remember the song that the SPLA sang its struggle "yhal ganob ma bekof men yum chakal yha yha inshala nemud malu" "(southerners are not afraid of the fighting and so what if we die!)". I love this song of struggle! I once sang it for a different occasion at the Sudanese Embassy in Romania in 1993, when Ahmed Swar el Dab and those in the embassy mistreated us.

Evidence of genocide and rape is countless. Although many people from Southern Sudan know this, foreign governments and NGOs estimate approximately two million people have lost their lives. No one can really give the exact number, and the truth remains that the Arabs' campaign of ethnic cleansing was to irradiate the black Africans from the main land.

Evidence of one episode of rape came from the Catholic Bishops Conference (SCBC) message to IGAD in the "South Sudan Post" of September 2000 (8th edition, page 10). The international community needs be made aware of this such evidence. We witness young girls, 13 or 14 years old, carrying babies born from cruel and humiliating acts of rape and abduction that will traumatise them for the rest of their lives.

My own testimony

On the 2nd of September 1986, I left Wau and headed to Khartoum. After three days of hardship, together with three friends we managed to reach Aweil. Prior to my departure, the military convoy left Wau on 1st September 1986 and was ambushed by our rebels between Wau and Aweil while travelling on the main road.

According to the information given to us by the rebels and local people whom we met on our way to Aweil, the army suffered severe losses and many soldiers lost their lives. In the one-hour attack 10 to 12 soldiers died; from their side three men lost their lives, and five more were injured.

This convoy arrived in Aweil a week later, after we had already arrived in town, and it was clear that the soldiers had truly been attacked. In addition, they had been attacked by bees and snakes, killing three men.

Killing people is not in my nature, but I congratulated our bees that day. You can see that even creatures in Southern Sudan consider Arabs their enemies and fight them wherever they find them.

While in Aweil the information about the attack was confirmed by a soldier named Heidar, whom I knew from Wau. Heidar said that indeed, they had lost 11 men, and seven others were wounded.

We spent nearly two weeks in Aweil waiting for the train to take us to Nayla; from there we would find our way to Khartoum. The train was carrying the remaining soldiers from the battalion destroyed by the SPLA in Tunj and Rumbek in early 1986. They travelled on that train together with their families; some were heading to Nayla, and others to Khartoum.

The SPLA is believed to have killed and captured many of these remaining battalions. Those heading to Khartoum where being led by Salva Chol Ayat (who was, by then, a brigadier in the Sudanese Army).

Every village, town, and hut along the railway from Aweil to Udhum, Wedeweil, Wathok, Ariath, Mabior, Maker (Rum-Aker), Malual and finally Agok station was burned to rubble; people were shot dead by the Sudanese Army. Mortars were shot into remote villages. I do not know how many innocents were killed out there.

One tragic incident, which none of us who travelling on that train will ever forget involved a returning soldier a southerner from Rumbek in the regiment heading to Khartoum. He had a brother who was mentally ill. On the ride between Malual and Mugalid, the soldier was disarmed and his sick brother was shot dead by an Arab soldier who claimed the victim was an agent of the SPLA.

After the holocaust of the Jewish nation in Europe in World War II, no other nation on earth had suffered as much as the people of Southern Sudan, although this is not to deny the Armenians' genocide at the hands of the Turks in from 1915 to 1917 or the Toto genocide in Rwanda. It is indeed an appalling situation that our nation has endured for centuries.

Our people were sold by the thousands into slavery, our lands were seized, and our girls and women were raped. Our homes were set on fire as the Arabs from the north took our livestock. Some of us were forced to accept Islam as our religion, claiming that we must change our name to a Muslim name in order to be holy the same ritual we encountered with Christianity in order to be baptised

Every southern family lost someone lovely, sometimes many people. Some were killed while fighting the government troops, while others were tortured or forced into domestic slavery in the northern cities.

We are a nation suffering through both a war and the false identity that has been imposed upon us. I remember Garang de Mabior saying that the Arabs want us to become Arabs and Muslims. Was God wrong when He made us blacks? Of course no one knows God's secrets and reason for creating the various races. Only God knows why He made us blacks and gave us this land to be ours! Southerners, we need a stronger unity than ever! The first civil war from 1955 to 1972, which ended with the Addis Ababa Agreement brought nothing to the south and the southern people; on the contrary, it brought us suffering and hardship.

According to the agreement, funds were supposed to be released and directed towards reconstruction and development of civil society. The same funds were used by the northern elite to buy our politicians.

Can you tell me how many hospitals, schools, clubs, universities, or roads were built with these funds?

A few projects were set up, but they were full of mis-calculation. For example, a fruit and beer factory (Masna Wau) was built in Wau; however, from an economical point of view, such a project cannot succeed without a full supply of raw materials and sufficient manpower. Wau was not a strategic place to build such a project as it lacked the raw materials necessary. The factory should have been constructed in the Azande area, where a steady supply of fruits exists throughout the year.

In reality, the idea was to satisfy the populations of Wau and Bhar el Ghazalian, as well as the whole south, so that people could be proud and say, "Look, we have a factory in Bhar el Ghazal."

At schools everywhere in the south, the short supply of teachers and educational materials had a profound effect. I remember in Malou, 12 miles from Rumbek, we were made to sit on stones and write on the ground at school. We had no books to use or chairs or benches to sit on, and the teachers had only one old teaching book on each subject, which they shared.

I believe they might have bought all the teaching materials from their own pockets not from the budget given to them by the government that was supposed to provide everything for the school.

The south's budget was lost in corruption, starting with the central government offices in Khartoum. The central government would use the money to divide our politicians so that they fought amongst themselves. When the money reached the southern offices, the big fish (those politicians in higher positions those known to us) would subtract their part before the little fish

We left from Marialbai (in the Aweil region) for Wau and settled in Zagolona (a local Arabic word meaning "they throw us out") near Griniti, where my brother-in-law's military headquarters unit was based.

I started Grinti Primary School in 1976 in Wau Bhar El Ghazal. This school was, and still is I believe, a military school where only soldiers' children or relatives can attend; 95 percent of the students were northerners and 5 percent were southerners. Only children or relatives of those in prominent positions attended this school, with fewer children coming from those southern soldiers' families.

We had almost everything that was needed for school, from books to pencils, blackboards, teachers, etc. When other schools were going on strike and experiencing shortages of teachers and school materials, our school was well off. This is just another example that illustrates how the south and southerners suffered after the Addis Ababa Agreement.

5.

Need for unity

Brothers and sisters, for years I have been asking myself why can we not unite? What prevents
our unity? Are there factors that cannot unite
us? To these questions, and many others, I would
like to give the best answer I can. These are my
personal beliefs, and I think that, if everyone
asks himself these questions and finds suitable
answers, our unity can go ahead.

Unity needs a core that defines what is unified. Without knowing the truth about us, there
can be no definition of unity. Southern unity
can only be possible when the unifying factor is
properly defined. To give you an idea, let me first
define the natural unity of a family.

Family unity is based on a natural relationship
(birth) and genetic and social factors, while personal unity is based on what individuals share or
have in common, such as skin, geographic location, physical features or appearances, and common enemies. Notice I do not mention language
as a factor because it is the only thing most of

us do not have in common due to our natural diversity.

If we carefully examine each of these factors, we can see that a lot more unites us than divides us. Let me start with the skin factor. Although some amongst us have lighter skin, we are all considered blacks those of us from Southern Sudan, I mean.

We all belong to Southern Sudan, so no one can deny the geographic location factor.

As far as our physical features or appearances, the majority of us are tall and lithe.

Our common enemies are the Arabs in northern Sudan.

The natural factors unite us more than the political agenda that divides us. I very much like the song "Africa Unite" from legendry Bob Marley I call it "South Sudan Unite." My words are in parentheses.

> "How good and pleasant it would be before God and man to see the unification of all Africans (of all southerners).

> Unite for the benefits of your (our) children.

> Emancipate yourself (ourselves) from the slavery.

We have been down in captivity (in slavery) so long."

If we unite, we will be free.

Let's all unite and make the south a home for everyone a home with no fears, but one of peace and tranquillity; a home without discrimination and ghost houses; a home where every citizen feels free.

We need to unite and emancipate ourselves from real slavery and from the long domination of the political arena, the Arab culture, the Arabic language, and all kinds of repression.

We need to unite and emancipate ourselves from being forced to accept the Arab identity.

We need to unite and emancipate ourselves from poverty and primitivism.

The whole world has advanced, even neighbouring Chad and Central Africa Republic, but we are left far behind.

Our unity is the key to resolving all of these issues. It is the key to our prosperity and the key to catching up with the world that is well ahead of us.

The time has come! Answer the knocking at every southern heart and at each door telling us

"Hey! You people have a duty, an obligation, and a responsibility to carry on."

Our society has suffered for a very long time from divisions created by colonist and northern elites to suppress us and to take away our dignity, values, and human rights. Brothers and sisters were turned against one another. Villages, towns, and tribes met the same fate. These divisions resulted in the political strife of Southern Sudan, and we have witnessed events during the previous two civil wars that divested and destroyed our society.

In order for us to stop any further aggression, we need a strong unity that must come first from our leaders. I insist on this point, owing to the fact that our leaders are responsible for the tearing up of the southern unity. They are the ones that have been dealing directly with the successive Khartoum governments. They are the ones that divided our society with their political agendas

Our unity must start in the form of dialogue among southerners; this is crucial. The aims of these dialogues should be to heal everyone's wounds and restore our values of fraternity and mutual respect, especially with our rival tribes. We cannot face our enemy if we are divided. We must forgive and reconcile with one another and be a united nation.

In the Holy Bible, St. Mathew, Chapter 5: verses 21-26, Jesus said:

> 21 "you have heard that people were told in the past, don't commit murder; anyone who does will be brought to trial. 22 But I tell you: whoever is angry with his brother will be brought to trial, whoever calls his brother you good-for-nothing! Will be brought before the council, and whoever calls his brother a worthless fool will be in danger of going to the fire of hell. 23 So if you are about to offer your gift to God at the altar and there you remember that your brother has something against you, leave your gift there in front of the altar, go at once and make peace with your brother, and then come back and offer your gift to God. 25 If someone brings a lawsuit against you and takes you to court, settle the dispute with him while there is time, before you get to court. Once you are there, he will hand you over to the judge, who will hand you over to the police, and you will be put in jail. 26 There you will stay, I tell you, until you pay the last penny of your fine.

The book of God advise us to forgive and reconcile with our brothers and sisters before we take a step forward and offer our gifts to got their shares. Finally, when the tiny remainder trickled down from the whole budget to the institutions, nothing much was left for hospitals or schools. That was how our institutions were functioning.

The same thing happened from 1983 to 2004, when most of the southern institutions were based in Khartoum. Everything from the budgets —down to a gram of sugar —was divided at the headquarters in Khartoum. Poor, average citizens got nothing.

I happened to be one of the luckiest pupils from the south enjoying six good years of primary education. My brother-in-law, Belabuk Thuj Kual Arub (may God bless him and let him rest in peace) married my sister Aphobo Watod, and both told my parents that they intended to take me with them to Wau, where they would enrol me in school. It was a bizarre idea and a hard decision for my family to accept because I was the youngest in the family. In those days in Southern Sudan, most parents would not let their children go to school or to town because they were afraid that their children would learn to steal or become vagabonds, shalouk (Arabic word for vagabond).

After a long debate, my parents (specially my mother) gave in and allowed my sister and her husband to take me.

God or before we can even go to court with a brother, owing that the consequences are likely to be higher. If you insist on offering to God your gifts without making peace and reconciling with an offended brother, God will not accept such gifts because He is a God of peace and forgiveness. You must make peace with your brother first.

If you do not settle your problems with him before going to court, you may end up in jail and serve a long jail term because the judge will find you guilty and hand you over to the police, who will keep their eyes on you.

So we need to build a consensus on the need to make our unity attractive to every southerner. It must be stronger than ever because we are strong nation. We must forgive and reconcile before facing our big devil and those who desire to destroy us. We must always be prepared in front of our enemies. If we go to the referendum without a clear objective, unprepared, then our fate will be in great danger and our nation will end up in slavery.

Let us not close the door of this opportunity. If we close it for the second time, then we are closing ourselves in for good and this time we cannot blame the north, only ourselves.

One day prior to the signing of the peace accord, I was discussing Sudan's problems with a friend from Darfur. This friend believes in the case of our people, so he said to me, "Santino, after six years, if you [southerners] do not say yes for the self-determination, then you are the most stupid people on earth!"

I totally agree with his point of view because a good student cannot fail the same exam twice unless there is something wrong with him. We are not stupid, only very selfish; everyone wants what is best for himself and for his family (nepotism).

I was very pleased when the South-to-South dialogue conference started in Nairobi on the 9th of April 2005. Although much of what was said (equal participation in power sharing and faire opportunities for everyone especially those in the movement who fought for 22 years) and promised by the leaders was not put into practice, it was good positive step forward.

Because of these wonderful people, we are now enjoying the benefits of peace. Peace is not possible without cost. They made sacrifices. Those who died (our martyrs) on the battlefields or who were assassinated must be remembered now and forever. Their precious blood should always unite and guide us and our coming generations. Those who are alive deserve to be honoured.

Since the foundation of our glorious movement in 1983, I have always been, and still am, one of its strongest supporters. As many of you did, and still do, I have supported the movement in every step both glorious and bad (in my personal views). The only way to get our rights was to fight the Arab government in Khartoum till the south was freed.

When millions of our brothers and sisters left their loved ones, their properties, and their jobs or studies and took whatever means they had in hand to fight the Arabs, they only had one clear thing in mind: liberate Southern Sudan from the Arabs and their government in the north. Those who gave their blood for the south to be free and for its people to be a free society defined clear objectives. A clear vision is really a picture of how things would be if you followed your plans.

During the struggle, one my most upsetting days was the day when our brothers defected from the SPLA/M on the 30th of August 1991 and started fighting one another instead of the enemy. It was a nightmare for the south and the southern people.

I was also deeply saddened whenever I heard of the elimination or disappearance of our politicians who simply disagreed with the SPLA/M leader.

I am not denying that there were some mistakes or damage done to the movement by both individuals as well as groups, but whatever the case, I condemn the killing of a southerner by another southerner. We southerners must not kill our brothers and sisters. Those who know me know how strong I am in condemning such actions.

While supporting the movement as many of you do, I have always objected to the idea of a "New Sudan" as laid out by its leader Garang de Mabior.

Sudan is old and will remain old forever if the northerners do not change their negative mentality about us.

An Eritrean leader who has lived in exile in Sudan for a long time during that country's own struggle for freedom from Ethiopia once remarked:

> Northern Sudanese Arabs regard themselves as first class citizens of Sudan; they regard non-Arab Muslims of Northern Sudan as second class citizens; any foreign Muslim nationals living in Sudan are third class citizens; South Sudanese then come as the forth class citizens.

> The only time a Northern Sudanese regards a South Sudanese as a fellow citizen of Sudan is when that South Sudanese concedes that he has no

political or even social ambition and that
the Northern Sudanese are his rulers[21]

This idea is absurd and against the will of
our people, who no longer will accept being want
considered the lowest class in their country.

During the 21-year struggle, I thought the
leader of the SPLA/M pushed this agenda forward in order to blackmail the Arab world that
supported regimes in Khartoum. I also thought
that, when the victory or right time comes, the
façade would be dropped and the real agenda (the
independence of southern Sudan) would be put
before, and supported by, all leaders. To make
sure I was not fooled by the latter thought, I dis-
cussed this issue with Pagan Amum and Yashir
Arman during their two visits to Paris in 2001
and 2002.

Arman supported the New Sudan idea, but
Amum re-assured me that he was supporting his
case like any other southerner. Amum said that
the leaders did not want to complicate the case
and have more enemies; however, when the right
time comes, our real agenda (self-determination)
will be on the table, and all our leaders will work
to achieve that goal.

He also said that it is going to be everyone's
responsibility, too, a belief I shared with him.

---

[21] Sudan's Latest Peace Agreement by Bona Malwal, page, 14.

As for Arman, I completely understood him saying he wants the New Sudan agenda simply because he is from the north. The only point that neither convinced me on was the SPLA/M alliance with the National Democratic Alliance (NDA) for the NDA are all Arabs and in the end will ally with their Muslim brothers rather than with us, as they have always done!

So much time was wasted making friendship with these northerners. That time should have been given to and invested in discussing unity with our defected brothers and with militias that were fighting along side the government. Here I would like to take the opportunity to provide three examples why I assert they are all Arabs:

1. Before the fall of Nimeiri in 1985, al-Shadiq advocated the inevitable Islamisation and Arabisation of Southern Sudan through the manipulation of southern leaders (we all know those whom al-Shadiq manipulated). In public statements made in Saudi Arabia after the power was taken from Nimeiri and in Iran shortly after becoming prime minister of the coalition government, al-Shadiq aligned himself with his Muslim brothers, calling for the expansion of Islam. He went on to criticise Nimeiri's laws as an affront to Islam, stating that these laws thus need to be replaced by those of Islamic principles (meaning all of Sudan should be ruled by

Islamic laws).

2. In al-Shadiq, coalition government, the Khatimiiya adopted even a harder line (position), stating that any concession to the regional autonomy or federalism in the south undermines the future of the Islamic state.

3. The National Islamic Front of al-Turabi is committed not just to Islam, but to a particular interpretation of Islamic law that includes the death penalty for apostasy[22].

I disagree with the point that the former chairman made about the right of self-determination when he said: "The challenge now for the government of Sudan is to make unity attractive to southern Sudan so that they vote for it during the referendum" (SPLM Chairman's 22nd Anniversary Address at a Mass Rally in Rumbek on 16th May 2005)

With respect to his Excellency and what he has achieved for us and for South Sudan and the southern people, I think this time he got it wrong. In my view, he should have said that the challenge now for the movement and its leadership is to make unity attractive to southern Sudanese so that they vote for the south during the

---

[22] Examples I, 2 and 3 see Root Causes of Sudan's Civil Wars, Douglas H. Johnson page, 79.

referendum. This is the goal of our people and should not be ignored by any leader.

I was going to ask his Excellency (the late Garang de Mabior) what sort of attraction he meant. Did he mean positions in the government at the national level (Government of National Unity), money and development? Or did he simply mean that, if the Arabs signed a peace accord, it would be the end of every myth?

I was going to remind him of what he said when he was asked on the 2nd of November 1987.

"Can you enlighten us as to why you were opposed to the Addis Ababa Agreement before you could see it operational?"

His answer follows:

> We were opposed to the terms of the Addis Ababa Agreement because its basic terms, and the basis for the agreement, were first to absorb the Anyanya into the national army, second to integrate it after absorption, and third to destroy it.

He was absolutely right, but recalling the terms of the past peace accord and the present one, what is the difference? For me, the difference is that the SPLA/M is wiser now than the previously. It added the self-determination agenda and the condition that the SPLA should not be absorbed into the national army. This is very much appreciated, and I can say bravo for such a great achievement.

The government's agreement to all points could also be seen as points of attraction by a government that will later break its promises when the right moment comes.

The point I want to make clear is that neither the National Islamic Front (NIF) nor any other incoming governments in Khartoum will keep its word. These factions have never kept their promises and will not do so in the future.

We are aware of the fact that what they declared and signed only remains in ink, so why waste our time beating around the bush. (Our objectives are like black ink on the white paper).

The leadership's responsibility is to pave the way so that the southern Sudanese have a healthy environment and go to the referendum with a fixed objective self-determination.

Our people took up their arms because of this solid and fundamental issue. They risked their lives so that our generation would no longer be considered second-class citizens. The struggle has been for freedom, liberty, equality, justice, and human dignity represented under democracy, which we have lacked for centuries. These values are inviolable and cannot be replaced with another system.

I acknowledge that the issue of unity amongst southern Sudanese is not an easy task for the leadership because of the long period of division and fratricide that has established negativity amongst us; we feel more like enemies than brothers and sisters.

Yet it is possible if our leaders (southern Sudanese leaders) are sincere.

Whenever and wherever two or more southerners meet, eventually a problem arises because we come from different backgrounds and different tribes. Fighting one another helps the north to destroy our society, both economically and socially. Why do we not learn from other societies that have the same human diversity and yet manage to unite behind their countries in one line politically as well as economically? The United States, Switzerland, and France are living examples. Numerous communities live together in these countries, which are the most advanced nations politically, socially, and economically.

This is not to say that these countries do not have their own problems, but they find a way to co-exist.

A citizen from these countries would care more about the present land than the country of his or her origin, I think.

In the United States, people of all races live together under the rule of law. In spite of their different political views and approaches, they all have one thing in common serving the United States and its national interests.

This should be our starting point. People and nations learn from one another. Let's adopt this strategy and be united for the south. Let's come together as one family and one nation (southern people) to love and respect one another and our leaders.

I know every southern community or tribe is based on mutual respect of families, and elders and caring for one another, as well as respect for the leaders.

These values are rare in many countries. Let's take advantage of these beautiful and wonderful values to build our new society.

I know some people will question this unity. In Upper Nile for example, the Dinka may question why they should accept unity when the Nuer (one of the largest tribes in Southern Sudan) have killed many people and loaded everything that they had on hand from livestock animals. The same question can be asked in Bhar el Ghazal, where Jur and Dinka may suggest revenge on Fertit (a group of Balanda, Ndogo, etc.) militias that have killed many, killing as many Fertits as possible, before talking about unity. The Equatorians, of course, would likely say the Dinka, Nuer, and others, will return again to dominate them so refuse this unity and remain divided to manage their our own affairs.

Here is what I say: Stealing, killing, and domination resulted from "divide and rule" policy. You may well remember every southerner in a high position who worked to bring his family, friends, and relatives into the office because of the empowerment of the corrupt government of Arabs in Khartoum. The militia killed our innocent people, whether in Wau, Malakal or Juba, were created and supported by the same government. They did it deliberately to divide us and weaken our unity so that we did not have the time to think and fix our eyes on them. They meant to destroy us, make us surrender and kneel before them, accepting Islam and becoming Arabs. Everything must be forgiven if we truly wish to live as brothers and sisters.

Brothers fighting one another come to reconcile and settle their problems at the end of the day. Let's first forgive one another and seek unity. If possible, let's stop using these identification codes, or words, such as Dinkawi or Gainqui (a Dinka), Blandwi (a Blanda), and Dour (Fertit in Dinka language).

Let's stop them indefinitely and replace them with general terms such as Bhar el Ghazalian or Equatorian.

Let us forgive one another and stop nepotism as well. I am sure our future will be guaranteed. When the Arabs in northern Sudan become our aggressors, we will easily respond and defeat them.

The Juba declaration on unity and integration between SPLA and the South Sudan Defence Forces (SSDF) is a historical event that our leaders, H. E Lieutenant General Salva Kiir Mayardit, First Vice President of the Republic of Sudan, Chief of Staff of Southern Sudan, Chairman of the SPLM, and Commander-in Chief of SPLA, and General Paulino Matip Nhial, President of the Government of SSDF, have struck, paving the way for other groups to join in building our country —southern Sudan. I would like to congratulate both leaders and those who have worked around the clock in achieving such an extraordinary deal. This once again demonstrates to us that everything is possible between brothers and sisters. It also sends a strong signal to the NIF and its northern brothers that our leaders have finally come to realise that dialogue is the only way out.

What a wonderful thing when brother fight brother and, at the end of the day before the sunsets resolves their differences.

What I really do not understand is why it took so long and so many lives to reach this deal done just now? What changed? Is this something coming from the hearts of the SSDF? Or is it a tactic by the INF to weaken the SPLA?

Whatever the answer, one thing is very clear: Both the SPLA and the SSDF have made history by turning the old page behind them. It is good that our brothers have come to realise that they do not have a safe haven in being with and serving the north. Southern Sudan is a safe place for every southerner.

I want to thank both leaders for their historic achievement. General Matip, you are the champion. You have gained every southerner's heart by leaving past hostilities behind you. I hope to see other groups joining in soon.

The recent agreement takes me back to what Professor David de Chand, Ph.D., Director for External Affairs/Spokesman SSUDA/SSDF (the external wing of the SSUDA/ SSDF), said when Garang de Mabior was killed

> "Let's also unite at this time of mourning and difficulty to re-strategize, reconstruct, and resolve the course of democracy, peace, nationalism, and national interest to pioneer the future for the people of Sudan and South Sudanese in particular. Let's continue the struggle for democracy, peace, liberty, freedom, equality, and social justice to move forward. There will be no retreat until victory is achieved. Our leaders,

including Dr. Garang de Mabior have died for their country and a just cause. Let's move forward together and united in times like these. The struggle continues, God bless you all[23].

As I already said, I was touched by these words. Now, as his declaration comes true, I can say I am not only touched, but also admire both men for being real leaders who mean what they say.

For years, I have heard people saying that the late Garang de Mabior was the only obstacle standing in the way of unity for the southerners. Now that he is gone, why have some not joined the SSDF and returned home? Brothers, you do not have time to waste. Pack your luggage now and come home. We have been waiting for you. South Sudan will never refuse its children. Do not waste your time and energy serving those in the north who exploit you and turn you against your people. Come home before the south declares you as its enemy. (In my view, anyone serving the Arabs in the north is an enemy of Southern Sudan.)

The south is ruining out of patience. Why you keep running away? How long will you be running? You cannot run away from your own people. Why shall you continue to live in such a negative way?

If you fear to lose your position, your right to being a Muslim, you must realise that the south and the southern people have not been fighting Islam or Mus-

---

[23] Source: www.gurtong.org, condolence Book.

lims. We are simply at war with those in the north who want to take a way our right of self-identity.

Do not ally yourselves with these evil people who show no mercy on our children and older people. Even if they take away everything and kill, they cannot take away our pride and love for southern Sudan. They cannot extinguish the flame that has been burning inside us.

6.

Unanswered question

In the wars of 1955 and 1983, which have dragged our country from its economic and political development, the people of southern Sudan fought not only for the self-determination and the sharing of power with northerners, but also for their own liberation from the issue of Sudan's identity, which the north has for so many decades imposed upon every Sudanese. It is about being Arabs and Muslim.

Northerners have sought to identify themselves both as Arabs and Muslims, which I personally approve of because I believe each person is free to choose his or her identity. Although I do not believe that they are Arabs, I respect their choice.

Southerners and some indigenous tribes identify themselves as Africans and do not want to be called Arabs. The northern elites imposed this identity on us without asking what the Sudanese people thought or wanted.

The failure from those who negotiated and signed the two peace agreements to address the latter issue may lead the country into another chaotic civil war if it is not carefully considered.

The Arabs in the north will not give up their right of being Arabs or Muslims; on the other hand, the southerners have not agreed to be called Arabs and will not accept being driven away from their African roots.

The sense of unity for the Arabs in northern Sudan is to have one Sudan united on the basis of Islam and the Arab culture, ignoring non-Muslims and non-Arabs. In another words, unity for northerners is to create a Sudan that is fully Islamised and Arabised, a Sudan without Christianity or other beliefs, a Sudan ruled under Islamic law (Sharia) and accepted by all Sudanese regardless of their beliefs or cultures.

So why not divide the country into two, north and south, and let people from both parts chooses their identity in a democratic way by —"referendum" and not by force?

As the history tells us, we the people of Southern Sudan have never been free to enjoy what other free nation have been enjoying —freedom in all its forms. We have not been able to enjoy our lives as a family or even to celebrate our national day as a free nation —a day that we do not have for the time being. The children of free nations (those countries that have full stability) are spending every minute of their lives enjoying that which freedom offers: freedom, education, sports, music etc. However, the children of Southern Sudan have been forced to waste their time living as refugees throughout the world due to the unrest caused and forced upon them by the Arabs in northern Sudan (those we have always identified as Jellabs). Our children have been born beyond the borders of their original homeland, suffering from discrimination and the problems outlined earlier. The generations before us spent their lives as refugees in many different countries instead of our homeland. We, in turn, suffer abroad, wasting our time seeking refugee status and labouring hard to survive.

Some of us have spent many years fighting to get refugee status or to resettle in countries where the peace and tranquillity that we do not have in our own country of Sudan exist. Some have succeeded in obtaining such status, but others still have their files stocked in a chest of drawers or are waiting for orders of deportation. We still do not know when we will be able to return home to our families, relatives, and friends. The real question now is why have we been suffering so much for so long when we still do not know what our fate (future) will be in 2011? (The year of the referendum, which is believed to be the decisive year for the future of Southern Sudan.) Who has caused us all these suffering? I think we know who and why.

Our fathers (elders) were not sleeping; they resisted and fought for our rights and freedom, from the Juba Conference in 1947 to the present.

Who have been fighting us? The Arabs in northern Sudan.

What do you think the solution is to this problem? Voting to separate the north and south in the referendum vote in 2011.

Who will vote? You, southerner! Only you can do it.

Who needs to pave the way and make it attractive for us? First, our politicians. Second, every individual citizen of Southern Sudan. Finally, the international community as well as our friends.

But how can that happen?

We must unite; it is the key to our independence. Our leaders must make it clear and let southern people know what we are going to vote for in 2011 and why.

I totally disagreed with the slogan (unity) use by the Arabs in northern Sudan and their allies in southern Sudan. Our elder politicians (Those who have loved and still love South Sudan) have fought to change things so that all Sudanese can live in unity and harmony (in the case, of Anyanya I), and yet nothing changed with the north blocking every dialogue. Lately, the SPLA/M has struggled with the same issues of freedom, equality, segregation, racism, discrimination, and nepotism, yet the situation is worsening. It's clear as day that the Arabs in the north have locked their minds and thrown out the key that opens all doors to any dialogue to resolve these fundamental issues that concern we southerners as well as other marginalised areas.

Brothers and sisters, the northerners cannot change and will never change their Islamic laws or accept Africans. We are dreaming to think we will have a democratic country! Can you name one Arabian country that has a democratic system? The Arabs in northern Sudan have not brought any such plan to the table. They have just broken and dishonoured the agreements they have signed and promised in the Comprehensive Peace Accord (CPA) that asserted in forming the government of the National Unity there would be a fair share of power.

Was that the case? No, of course not. SPLA/M struggled to get the Ministry of External Affaires and the rest of the deputies.

Let me ask you southerners, who among you believed in unity with the north? Where is the unity they talk about? Can you see that the regime in Khartoum has made separation more attractive to the southerners rather the unity of

Sudan? Bashir and his northern colleagues have only defined what southern will vote for when they killed our beloved leader Garang de Mabior and our people in Khartoum and Cairo in 2005. In 2011, if you vote for the separation, then you make an excellent choice to avert another Any-anya. It means lasting peace in Sudan.

When you cast your vote make sure you vote for separation and not unity.

Thank you not only for bringing freedom to Southern Sudan, but also for making Africa a better place.

As for me, do not worry. I am casting my vote now. I am for the independence of our beloved Southern Sudan.

Here is my vote.

Voting card	
Referendum of 2011	
✓	Independence of Southern Sudan
	Unity of Sudan

Note for publisher: This is just an example. You can draw a better one

7.

The killing of Dr. John Garang de Mabior

On August 6, 2005, the new SPLM leader, SALVA Kiir, Addressed mourners during the funeral service for the late rebel leader and first vice president John Garang in Juba, southern Sudan.

"Dear compatriots, the tragedy of our leader has strengthened our resolve to remain united as a movement and people. This is the best way the SPLM can honour its fallen hero".

I want once again to express my shock and deepest sorrow at the untimely death of our national hero and beloved son of Southern Sudan Dr. John Garang de Mabior, the former First Vice President of Sudan and the President of the Government of Southern Sudan.

I convey my prayers and heartfelt condolences to his wife, Mrs. Rebecca de Mabior, and his children; to the people of southern Sudan; to the Movement and its leadership; and to those who have lost their loved ones in riots from the peaceful protests against the killing of their leader.

I was at work when the news about his helicopter crash appeared on every news channel. My wife Gabriela told me the awful truth as I entered our home: "Look, Santino. There is bad news that has just come in. Bakery (a friend of mine) phoned and told me that John Garang has died!" It was like a terrible dream —I couldn't believe it. After a few seconds to think about the news, I rushed to the dining room to turn on the TVC.

First I tuned into Aljazeera; indeed, the event was on the screen. I knew immediately that the Arabs had got him for I knew the Arabs would not let him stay in Khartoum (based on the fact that the Arabs kill southern intellectuals). My second though was to the future of Southern Sudan without him and what SPLA/M leadership would decide!

This time became a true test for the southern people and our leaders. We are now a nation in the deepest crisis —we are a nation facing an uncertain future. The death of Garang de Mabior has humiliated every southerner (both his supporters and his opponents) and jeopardised the Peace Agreement with the Sudanese Government signed by him on the 9th of January 2005. He served as symbol of hope to both us southern Sudanese and to the millions of marginalised people of Sudan: Nuba Mountains, Blue Nile, Darfur, and Eastern Sudan. The Arabs think that by killing him, just as they did William Deng, Father Saturino, and many others; they killed our hope.

The got it wrong.

The Southern nation will continue the vision for southern nationalism laid out by our murdered politicians until every last vision is accomplished. Nothing will stop us from our quest —the quest for a southern place, an identity and dignity that our late hero Garang de Mabior gave. He gave it his best, fighting for it for half his life.

At this sad and terrible moment in our long history with the north, we the citizens of southern Sudan should stand hand in hand in solidarity and unite behind our cause. Garang de Mabior has died, but our cause for freedom, justice; equality, fraternity and democracy have not. We are endowed with people who, no doubt, will continue to carry on our mission. The killing of our brother should unite and guide us. There is no time for us to waste. Any personal agenda that is against southern Sudan and its people must be stopped immediately.

Our unity at this stage should be at the top of every southerner's agenda. Our destiny as a notion is at risk. As CDR Salva said in his speech, "the tragedy of our leader has strengthened our resolve to remain united as a movement and people. This is the best way the SPLM can honour its fallen hero"[24]. The only way we can honour him, and those who have already gone ahead of him, is by strengthening ourselves and uniting.

As I was reading the book of condolences written by our brothers and sisters on the Gurtong website, I found an interesting entry by Professor David de Chand, PhD, Director for External Affairs/Spokesman SSUDA/SSDF (the External wing of the SSUDA/ SSDF). I was touched by all of the entries, but this one in particular touched my heart and filled my eyes with tears. It was so special because it came from a group who still have their guns. Professor David wrote:

> For South Sudanese everywhere, we pray that you know Dr. Garang's spirit and the spirit of those before him would always be part of our dreams and the country they loved. Let their will live and be done to augment the cause of democracy, freedom, liberty, peace and social justice that they so cherished and worked so hard to attain. This is the time to mourn, reflect and pray for guidance and a new beginning. Let's all take this time humbly to make reflections on reconciliation and to forgive one another and to move

[24] Source: www.gurtong.org, August 6, 2005.

forward with the process peace, love and brotherhood in our hearts, minds and souls.

Let's also unite at this time of mourning and difficulty to re-strategize, reconstruct and resolve the course of democracy, peace, nationalism and national interest to pioneer the future for the people of Sudan and South Sudanese in particular. Let's continue the struggle for democracy, peace, liberty, freedom, equality; and social justice to move forward. There will be no retreat until victory is achieved. Our leaders, including Dr. Garang de Mabior have died for their country and a just cause. Let's move forward together and united in times like these. The struggle continue, God bless you all (Gurtong website).

Thank you very much, brother. Our struggle must continue till we prevail. With your words you have touched the core of our weakness. If we unite, our glorious victory is inevitable; it is the only weapon that is lacking in achieving our ultimate victory. Let's use this tragic moment to unite.

The whole world, especially those who espouse peace, was shocked by this incident, but I can tell you —do not be surprised. Southerners are accustomed to the brutal killing of their leaders by northerners. This list of those killed is long. As long as the south is tied to the north, the killing of Garang de Mabior will not be the last. More are likely to die if our remaining leaders do not make an immediate move to stop this genocide and ruthless killing of our people.

In the North itself, NIF has already proven to be one of the ruthless ruling military powers in the history of Sudan. Since it coup d état on the 30th of June 1989, its members have killed many officers from the Sudanese army who they claimed were engaged in or planning a military coup against the group's progress. The killing included their own colleagues in the National Salvation Revolutionary Command Council (NSRCC). Omar el Bashir killed Brigadier Mohammed Salih al-Zubayer, the deputy chairman of the Revolution Command Council, and Shams al-Din in a similar manner as what he used to kill Garang de Mabior: a plane crash.

In the South, the current regime of NIF has been followed their fathers' agenda, which is killing southerners till they all surrender and accept Islam and the Arab identity. The first victim was Brigadier Pio Yukwan Deng, a Shilluk who was a commander in Kapoeta in 1976, whom they poisoned on the 11th of September 1991. I am not sure when exactly he was killed?

Both NIF and el Bashir had a number of reasons to eliminate Garang de Mabior. He was a southern intellectual and leader of a victorious revolution against their government, including their own regime, for 21 years. The northerners have been waiting patiently for him for 22 years. His military and political qualifications made him a strong leader who succeeded in many achievements, such as leading the movement, remaining the first southern Sudanese leader whom they government of Khartoum has not managed to deceived, and signing the peace accord. Northerners saw their future in danger when the victorious Garang de Mabior came to Khartoum on the 8th of July 2005 after 22 years of absence. Millions of people came out en mass to receive true leader, the one who had given up his pleasant life in Khartoum 22 years earlier and escaped to the bush to lead a guerrilla war against what he considered his people's oppressors (the Arabs and their governments).

The northerners did not want Garang de Mabior to humiliate them in the country's first election under the peace accord, which Garang de Mabior was more that likely to win, becoming the first Christian and indigenous black African president in Sudan's history. With his many victories over the Sudanese government both military and politically, Garang de Mabior had humiliated every northern government and leader, including Nimeiri, retired General Abdel Rahman Swar al-Dahab, Asadiq el Mahdi and Omar el Bashir all of whom vowed to crack down and destroy the movement. Garang de Mabior managed to turn northerners against one other in the case of Turabi and Bashir.

NIF and el Bashir also wanted to dishonour the current peace accord, which they were forced into by the international community. They though that killing Garang de Mabior would create considerable challenges for SPLA/M leadership, who would fight for positions, eventually leading to civil war and another division amongst southerners. This situation would provide a great opportunity to continue convincing the world that the south is not yet ready to rule itself.

Fifthly, the NIF wanted send a signal to SPLA/M's leadership: "Look! We got your headman. It will be your turn if you do not do what we say, so pay close attention. We can kill you as well" killing Garang de Mabior would lead southerners and their leaders to relinquish fighting.

Whatever the reasons, the fact remains that they brutally killed Garang de Mabior. The fact remains that southerners are fed up, and the absolute majority thinks that the south must break away. The fact remains that Kiir's new SPLA/M administration will continue fighting and defending the cause of Southern Sudan. His successor will continue to do so. My advice to northerners is to let the south go peacefully. You are fighting a very poisonous snake. If you do not let them go peacefully, they will be forced to kill you and leave. No one wants to reach such a position. If the south break away by force, the south and north would never have good neighbouring relations.

You killed Garang de Mabior, and with him you buried any unity. He was your partner for unity. Adieu unity!

Garang de Mabior died with our unarmed and innocent brothers in different Sudanese cities. They were simply showing their sympathy and supporting their leader. They were mowed down by the Islamic government police and army. These people fought for a good cause and against the NIF's dirty business with the blacks. They were freedom fighters. May God bless Garang de Mabior and all those who have fallen after him.

Even after Garang de Mabior was buried, a number of people continued to be killed. The imams used the mosques' microphones to call people for jihad with the knowledge of the government, which armed people to kill southerners. The media was also silent about these atrocities. For years the people of Southern Sudan have been trying to fathom the mysterious nature that allowed the killing of their citizens in such a way.

8.

What our leaders ought to do

Both SPLA/M and another Southern Sudanese parties must now directly address to desire of most southern Sudanese that the only way to free themselves and end their sufferings is to break away from the north and have their own country. They must say it in public so that our people are ready and vote for secession. Don't mix your personal agenda with that of the nation's desire. I know you don't *need* to teach because our people already know the lesson of living with Arabs. But it is important that you teach and now.

- Think more about your people and they will think more about you. If you give your best time and think about your people's needs —their pains their future —they, in turn, will think, love and serve you faithfully.

- You might have fooled the whole World

and reaped the rewarded, but your rewards will not last forever, especially if you have killed and buried your people's desires for independence. Don't ever shut down your people's will. Do what the majority of your people want.

- If you want to get, and maintain, good performance, you must let people know your outlook and that you care about the things they need. Share your thoughts with them. Tell your people what you intend to do and your reasons for doing so. Reassure them about their future, but do not insist on doing anything they do not want.

- You get from people only what you deserve. They will pay you back in the same way that you have treated them.

- If you want your people to be responsible, be responsive to their needs. If you want your people to listen to you and do what you ask, first respond to their needs.

- Eleanor Roosevelt said, "No one can make you inferior without your permission". You politicians, with your tolerance, have made Southern Sudan inferior. You gave the north the permission. Now it is time to take responsibility. Look at your people, listen to their needs, and act in their interests.

- It takes time and practice to achieve specific goals. Give yourself time and space and think twice before taking one step forward.

- Good performance starts with clear goals. Define your objectives first before looking for the ways to achieve your goals.

An open letter

My dear fellows from Southern Sudan,

Let me take this great opportunity to salute all of you, wherever you are, in the name of our beloved Southern Sudan, remembering our brave boys, girls, mothers and old men who sacrificed their lives for us all and for the South.

Today, and for the second time in our history, we live in a new era of peace, but a very fragile one because of the past experiences with the governments in Khartoum. The actual peace is a historic moment and a great chance and opportunity that our people have not had for a half a century. It contains the right to exercise the self-determination in five years. Let's all rejoice, but be very cautions.

You know that getting this chance was never an easy task. We paid the highest price ever in order to have it; children and mothers suffered unbearably as well as our old men. Unfortunately, some have not lived to see the fruits of what they have fought or suffered for. My respect and thoughts will always be with them.

By their precious blood, they lifted up on high our names and our dignity and made us a glorious nation. Will there be recompensing for what they have done for us? Will there be respect to honour their names from now and forevermore?

I think the most precious gift that that each one of us can give them is to say **Yes** to the independence of Southern Sudan and **No** to the unity of one Sudan on that historical day of referendum in five years' time.

Amshi yah abid ("Go you slave"). You, brothers and sisters, know very well what I am talking about. It is what the Arabs in the north (Awlad el balad) call the black Africans the southerners, the Nubians, and all indigenous groups.

Are you prepared again to accept their humiliating terms? Are you prepared to accept a second-class citizenship in a country that is totally yours? Are you prepared to live with the northerners who say non-Muslim or Abeed (blacks/Christian) cannot become president to rule wad el balad? Are you prepared to accept lower positions, such as the ministering to animals, when you are well qualified even to lead the country?

Thank you for saving Southern Sudan.

Long live Southern Sudan —long live to our suffering nation and blessed be those who died in the struggle!

Sincerely yours,

Santino F. Watod

Here i have taken out the list.

I would like to provide a list of those killed by different regimes in Khartoum during the two previous civil wars[25].

[25] Source: http://lokeji6.tripod.com/massacre/juba92.html

List N° 1

Names of those massacred in Wau at the wedding party:

N°	Name	Occupation
1	Dr Justin Papiti Akol	Vet Officer BGP
2	Victor Bol Bol	Executive Officer
3	Salvatore Kuol Mkual	Game/ Fisheries Officer
4	Gabriel Akon	Lab Assistant
5	Nyal Agoth	Book-keeper
6	Inyasio Madut Yai	Hides Assistant Officer
7	Paul Pap Majok	Book-keeper
8	Ottavio Deng Maroro Rehan	Head Clerk (One of the Two bridegrooms)
9	John Malual Thongian	Asst Hides Officer
10	Mayor Deng Kual	Book-keeper

11	Benjamin Bol Tiel	Book-keeper
12	Federick Abuok Deng	Book-keeper
13	Joseph Luk Aguek	Book-keeper
14	Henry Ring Duar	Book-keeper
15	James Marial Manyiel	Book-keeper
16	Nicholus Cor Malek	EX MP
17	Daud Chagai	Sudan Airways Officer
18	Joseph Dani	Medical Asst
19	Cypriano Cier Reham	Businessman
20	Majok N	Inspector
21	Mayen	Inspector
22	Ring Mabouc	Inspector
23	Henry Athuay Ayak	Int. Teacher
24	Andrew Yai Bol	-
25	Lawrence Malith Ring	Male Nurse
26	Athuai Maluil	Male Nurse
27	Samuel Agany Kuanyin	EX MP
28	Santino Ring Juk	Student

29	Salvatore Biar Ayac	Student
30	Mangar Nyol Aguok	Student
31	Thon Ater	Tribal Chief
32	Robert Wit	Student
33	Kamilo Martin	Political Cadre SFP
34	Francis Ring Ajak	Student
35	Doka Morgan	Businessman
36	Hamid Daud	Businessman
37	Barnaba Bak	Businessman
38	Yak	Businessman
39	Ring Henry Ring Jr.	4 years old
40	Ms. Maria Benjamin	-

The following list provides the names of the Security Officials and Civilians who disappeared in Juba between June and August 1992.

[In June and July 1992, the SPLA forces mounted major assaults on Juba, nearly captured the town. In the immediate aftermath of the attacks and in the weeks that followed, government forces responded by extra-judicially executing civilians and the captured SPLA soldiers during house-to house operations and arresting over 260 soldiers, police officers, prison guards paramilitary forces and prominent civilians.

I was there when all these happened. These people are not just names and figures as you see here. I knew many of them personally. To me, they are not just 300 cases of "disappearances"; every name I read, I see the person who was my neighbour, my uncle, my brother, my sister, my father, my teacher, my model, my friend... and behind them I see the families they left behind, the orphans and the widows [26].]

[26] Source http: //lokeji6.tripod.com/massacre/juba92.html

List N°2

—Police————————————

1. Major Gabriel Bazia

2. Capt Arkangelo Yugu

3. Sgt Khamis Alili

4. Col Daniel Kenyi [biographies not yet been gathered]

5. Sgt Major Awad Lemi Lako

6. Maj. Andrew Nathaniel Yigga

7. Lt Col Philip Modi

8. Wrt Off Andrew Lako

9. Lt Col Peter Lado

10. Maj Wilson Sometimes

—Arrest/disappearance not acknowledged by the government————

1. Maj. Wilson Namitti

2. Silas Amin Wani

3. Sgt Maj Awad Abbas

4. Leth Nhial Yakeny

5. Abdallah Ayoub Makuac

6. Arkangelo Morris Logolanyo

7. Khemis Daoud

8. Silvestro Laxo

9. Clement Kwoja Elia

10. Ismail Zakariah Hassan

—Wildlife

1. Capt Simon Samuel

2. Simon Jada

3. Lieutenant Nixon Lemi

4. Colonel James Peter Duling

5. Lieutenant Gerry Gadi

6. Lieutenant Raphael Onorato

7. Captain Henry Mawa Samuel- released

8. 1st Lt. Mark Taban Quirino-released

9. Lt Saleh

10. Lt Phlip Khamis

11.Lt Daniel Gajou

12.Lt Joseph Gaijuk

—Disappearance not acknowledged by the government —————

1. Capt Isaac Losuba

2. Major Francis Wani

3. Simon Sangya Ibrahim

4. Capt Nathaniel Jada

5. 1st Lt Lado Sule

6. Lt Col George Oketch

—Prisons————————————

1.

Maj. Pitia Kenyi Lado

2. Capt Francis Lemi Lado

3. Lt Lino Wani Lado

4. Sgt Jinaba Maranga

5. Sgt George Wani

6. Corp. John Wani

7. Corp. Michael Jeremano

8. Corp. Paulino David

9. W.Officer Valentino Lafatoi

10. Maj. Repent Juma

11. Cpt. Mohammed Khamis Sale

12. Lt. Simon Sanya

13. Sgt. Faustino Asu

14. Corp. Joseph Lubang

15. Corp. Augustino Taban

16. Corp. Luka Mazinga

17. Corp. George Lado

18. W.Officer Paulino Lado

19. Capt. Kamillo Koma Silas

20. Capt. Lazarus Joel Moni

21. Sgt. Joseph Amin

22. Sgt. Julian Yangi

23. Corp. Scopas Gali

24. Corp. Benty Boyi

25. Corp. John Baptista

26. Corp. Emmanuel Lado

27. W.Officer Benson Oyet

28. Capt. Joseph Taban Nimaya

29. Capt. Edward Wani Dere

30. Sgt. Babikir Tombe

31. Sgt. Nicolas Sebit

32. Corp. James Taban

33. Corp. Angelo Wani

34. Corp. Paulo Okot

35. W.Officer John Manna

36. W.Officer Daniel Agoyi

—Arrest/disappearance not acknowledged by the government—————

1. Col. Anania Lopu

2. Kamilo Anthony

3. Sergeant Milo Jamal

1. **Army**

2. Yohanna John Bedo

3. Daniel Majok William

4. Makur Marial Makur

5. Major Anyuat Nhial

6. Lt. Colonel Elias Lino

7. Sgt Major Ali Gore

8. Major Yohannes

9. Benjamin Malual Tek

10. Valentino Wani Alijo

11. Major Macut Thon

12. Major Andrew Aciek

13. Thelphiny Kulang Ader

14. Mjor Joseph Ladu

15. Major Zacharia

16. Major Andrew Mackec [unaccounted for]

—Civilians—

N°	Name	Occupation
1	Evelino Modi	Technician at Juba airport
2	Mustafa Abdel Gadi	Airport technician
3	Paulino Qumat	Pharmacy assistant
4	Francis Tombe	Student
5	Kenedy Khamis	Customs officer
6	Faustino Modi	Assistant executive officer
7	Tony Ilario [biographies not yet been gathered]	Member town council
8	Raimondo Pitya	Architect
9	Sarafino Pitya	Accountant
10	Alfred Yoron Modi	Radio Juba employee
11	Kenedy Lomeling	Customs officer
12	Wani Kabulu	Inspector of accounts
13	Eliseo TAban	Director, forestry department
14	Joseph W.D Wai	Geologist
15	Sebit Darfur	Tax officer
16	Katir James	Forester
17	Hillary Duku	[Escaped and fought for New Sudan]

18	Stephen Daniel	Veterinary surgeon
19	John Kabulu	-
20	Nicholas Jenario	Bank employee
21	Paul Alphonse	Engineer
22	Joseph Lako	Trader
23	Juma Albino [biographies not yet been gathered]	Prize control officer
24	Camillo Odongi Loyuk	Retired army brigadier and former governor of Eastern Equatoria (tortured to death).

—Victims of unknown occupation—

Victims with Unspecified Occupation- Police/wildlife/prisons/army

1. Lt. Col. Methodia Otone

2. Capt. Pompeo Abdallah

3. 1st.Lt. El-Haj Hussein

4. 1st.Lt. William A. David

5. Sgt.Maj Atilioa Okwari

6. Corp. Oliver Mada

7. L/Corp. Cossiano Lochobe

8. L/Corp. Valentino Ofera

9. L/Corp. Hillary Dominic Abdalla

10. L/Corp.Ben Oachi Acafido

11. L/Corp. Eliado Otuli Ogun

12. Lt. Keleto Lodiang Okwang

13. Lt. Joseph Wani

14. Maj. Andrew Nathaniel Issa

15. W.Officer Henry M. Ganzi

16. W.Officer Peter Maring

17. Sgt Maj. Terencio Locha

18. Sgt Maj. Ibrahim Khamis

19. Sgt. Liwa John

20. Sgt. Vinansio Jume

21. Sgt. John Salvatore

22. Corp. Marco Ija

23. Corp. Pio Lima

24. Corp. Solomon Ohire

25. L/Corp. Wani James

26. L/Corp. Peter Soro

27. Maj. Ruba Gamae

28. W.Officer Arkangelo Pitia

29. W.Officer John Manao

30. W.Officer Patrisio Wani

31. Sgt Maj. Suliman Lado

32. Sgt. Saturlino Kuang

33. Sgt. Julius Randi

34. Corp. Joseph Lado Lobang

35. Corp. Joseph Tombe

36. Priv. George Lado Jokke

37. Capt. Wondo Robert Yona

38. 1st Lt Mark Lado Tom

39. 1st Lt. Benjamin Anozai Golo

40. W.Officer Martin Oluma

41. Sgt. Gabriel Pitia

42. L/Corp. Rems Ira

43. L/Corp. James Oburak

44. L/Corp. Peter Bortel

45. L/Corp. Abdu Ochan Biajo

46. L/Corp. Pious Oketta Martin

47. Lt. Clement Loboyong

48. Lt. Sabasio Jekino Manyang

49. Lt. Timothy Wani Modi

50. W.Officer Amos Lako

51. W.Officer Kerubino Patrick

52. W.Officer John Atari

53. Sgt Maj. Lajeno Wani

54. Sgt. Jino Lomor-Moi

55. Sgt. Stanley Kenyi

56. Corp. Luka Mujinga

57. Corp. Clement Michael

58. Corp. Peter Lolik

59. Corp. Khamis Ramadan

60. L/Corp. Wani Abdullah

61. L/Corp. Cosmas Kenyi

62. Corp. Ananias Lagul

63. W.Officer Albert Mahmud

64. W.Officer Filanto Leptol

65. W.Officer Rephael Kissinga

66. Sgt Maj. Charles Baby*

67. Sgt. Francis Otto

68. Sgt. Gamal Milio

69. Sgt. Peter Maya

70. Corp. Michael Jarm

71. Corp Paul Kwaje

72. Augustino Swaka

—Civilians executed——————————

1	Mark Loboke Jenner	EC official
2	Andrew Tombe	USAID official
3	Aboudan Talle	USAID official
4	Michael Muto Atai	UN official

CREDENTIALS

My name is Santino Fardol, I was born in 1968 in Marialbai Aweil County in Southern Sudan. I began school in 1976 at Griniti Primary School, then attended Wau alif Scondray School. Due to the escalation of violence in Southern Sudan, I moved to Khartoum in 1986 to continue my studies; I studied at Maridi High School, and Berber School, where I sat for the final examinations and obtained a Sudan Certificate.

In January 1992, I was forced to leave Sudan, exiled to Romania. Because of my political views and beliefs regarding civil wars in Sudan, I was imprisoned with seven other colleagues from Southern Sudan by the Sudanese Embassy in Romania between 1993 and 1994. I was later acquitted in 2000, I graduated from the Academy of Economics Studies at Bucharest University.

Born during a troubling time in Sudan's history, I was taught by my father to love country, Southern Sudan, and my people and do whatever I could to liberate my country. Since I was child, I have believed that Southern Sudan has nothing in common with its northern counterpart. My desire has been to separate my country and my people from north's domination so that we southerners can live in absolute peace and freedom.

EPILOGUE

This book has been a labour of love and beliefs. It has been challenging, and I have had a number of setbacks in the process. I have had to rewrite it many times, especially after the death of the late hero Dr. John Garang de Mabior and the many challenges that followed.

I have suffered from a lack of information. I became sad and unable to concentrate on my writing when the news came in about my sister's death, yet I continued on and never gave up on the subject.

As millions of southerners read this book, I pray to God that I have reached my objectives. My first objective was to bring the memory of the past events to mind. I hope this book has been able to renew your belief in our long struggle with the north.

My second objective was to share with all of you my love of my (our) country and my (our) people, letting you to see the picture of my broken heart beyond what I put down on paper.

Finally, and most importantly, I wanted to provide an account and information that will influence your decision in the 2011 referendum. I hope that the useful information and reasoning provided in this book have justified why I insisted on Southern Sudan breaking away.

I am so thankful for what father has taught me.

I will be happy and rejoice when my people are free.

ABOUT THE BOOK

Since Sudan gained its independence from the British on the 1st of January 1956, the northerners have dominated the political arena of the country and make Islam the only legal religion (law), ignoring all other religions such as Christianity and other local beliefs.

Since then, the war in Sudan has worsened and continues to do so at an alarming rate. Watching the news on our TVs and reading the newspapers for the past 22 years and even nowadays in Darfur, Eastern Sudan, we are increasingly made aware of the genocides of the people in Southern Sudan and other marginalised areas.

Slavery and holy war have been declared against the South. Millions have been killed or displaced throughout the world. Others have undergone humiliation, surviving in the worst human conditions in shantytowns around Khartoum and other northern major cities. No one can really predict the end of the suffering of people of Southern Sudan.

Now the choice is ours. Do we accept slavery or become free men? Vote for the independence of Southern Sudan in the referendum.